SPOTLIGHT ON SPACE SCIENCE

JOURNEY TO MERCURY

MARY WILSON RHODES

New York

Published in 2015 by The Rosen Publishing Group, Inc.
29 East 21st Street, New York, NY 10010

First Edition

Editor: Susan Meyer
Book Design: Kris Everson

Photo Credits: Cover (main), pp. 13, 19, 21, 23, 25, 29 NASA; cover (small Mercury image), p. 11 NASA/Johns Hopkins University Applied Physics Laboratory/Carnegie Institution of Washington; p. 5 ESA/NASA/SOHO; p. 7 NASA/JPL-Caltech; p. 9 CLAUS LUNAU/Getty Images; p. 15 ESA; p. 17 Alan Dyer/Visuals Unlimited, Inc./Getty Images; p. 27 NASA/Johns Hopkins University Applied Physics Laboratory/Carnegie Institution of Washington/National Astronomy and Ionosphere Center, Arecibo Observatory.

Library of Congress Cataloging-in-Publication Data

Rhodes, Mary.
Journey to Mercury / by Mary Rhodes.
p. cm. — (Spotlight on space science)
Includes index.
ISBN 978-1-4994-0372-5 (pbk.)
ISBN 978-1-4994-0401-2 (6-pack)
ISBN 978-1-4994-0420-3 (library binding)
1. Mercury (Planet) — Juvenile literature. 2. Mercury (Planet) — Exploration — Juvenile literature. I. Rhodes, Mary. II. Title.
QB611.R48 2015
523.41—d23

Manufactured in the United States of America

CPSIA Compliance Information: Batch #CW15PK: For Further Information contact Rosen Publishing, New York, New York at 1-800-237-9932

CONTENTS

SCORCHED BY THE SUN

CHAPTER 1

Many millions of miles (km) from Earth is a battered, sun-scorched world called Mercury. This tiny **planet** is **orbiting** the Sun at an average speed of 31 miles per second (50 km/s).

From Earth, the Sun is a warming, yellowish-white ball of light in the sky. From the surface of Mercury, it's a very different story, because Mercury is the closest planet to the Sun. If you could stand on Mercury's surface during the part of its orbit when it is closest to the Sun, the Sun would appear three times larger than it does from Earth and over 10 times brighter! If you were standing on Mercury during the day, you would experience a scorching heat of 800°F (427°C).

Mercury is the smallest planet in the **solar system** and is only slightly larger than Earth's moon. If you can imagine the Earth as a baseball, little Mercury, by comparison, is just the size of a golf ball.

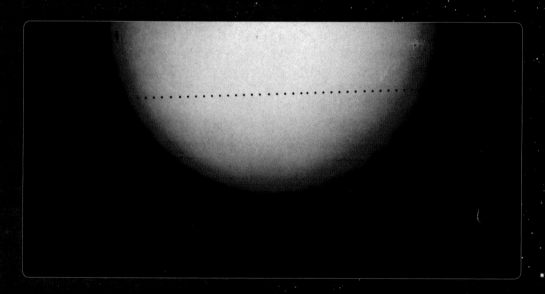

This photo shows Mercury's transit across the Sun in 2006. The tiny dots are Mercury at different positions. The large dark spot to the left is a sunspot.

THE FORMATION OF MERCURY
CHAPTER 2

About five billion years ago, Mercury did not exist. Earth, Mars, all the other planets in our solar system, and even the Sun were yet to be born.

The chemical ingredients to make the Sun and everything in the solar system did exist, though. These ingredients were floating in space in a **nebula**, which is a cloud of gas and dust.

Then, part of the cloud began to collapse on itself, forming a massive rotating sphere, or ball. A disk formed around the sphere from the remaining gas and dust. The material in the sphere was pressed together by **gravity**, causing pressure to build. As pressure built, the sphere's core heated up, reaching temperatures of around 18,000,000°F (10,000,000°C). Finally, the heat and pressure became so great that the sphere ignited, and a star was born. This new star was our Sun.

Gas and dust continued to spin in a disk around the newly formed star. Over time, this material clumped together, forming Mercury, Earth, and all the other planets and objects in the solar system.

Solar systems are formed from spinning gas and dust pulling together over time.

HOW VAST IS THE SOLAR SYSTEM?

CHAPTER 3

From our position here on Earth, it can be hard to imagine the vastness of our solar system. There is a fun way, however, to experience the scale of the solar system and visualize the size of the planets in comparison with each other.

If you take a bowling ball and imagine that it is the Sun, then small planets such as Mercury and Mars and the **dwarf planet** Pluto could be represented by pinheads. Venus and Earth would be the size of a peppercorn. Uranus and Neptune would be the size of a coffee bean, while Saturn would be the size of a marble, and giant Jupiter the size of a chestnut.

To match the scaled-down dimensions of the solar system, tiny pinhead Mercury would be about 10 yards (9 m) from the bowling ball Sun. The peppercorn Venus would be 9 yards (8 m) past Mercury, and Earth would be 7 yards (6 m) past Venus. Keep going with Mars, Jupiter, Saturn, Uranus, and Neptune. Finally, pinhead Pluto would be located just over 1,000 yards (914 m) from the bowling ball Sun. That's about the same length as 10 football fields!

Tiny Mercury is the planet with the closest orbit to the Sun.

MERCURY'S LAYERS

CHAPTER 4

Just like Earth, Mercury's inner structure is made up of three different layers.

Inside the planet is a huge core of iron that makes up about 80 percent of the planet's **mass**. The iron core is partially **molten** and has a radius of about 1,100 miles (1,800 km) from the center of the planet.

Surrounding the core is the mantle. This layer of molten rock is up to 400 miles (650 km) thick. The outer crust of the planet is a thick layer of rock 180 miles (300 km) deep, covered by gray rocks and dust.

Mercury has less mass than Earth, so the gravity on its surface is only about 38 percent of the gravity we experience on Earth. This means if you weigh 100 pounds (45 kg) on Earth, you would weigh only 38 pounds (17 kg) on Mercury.

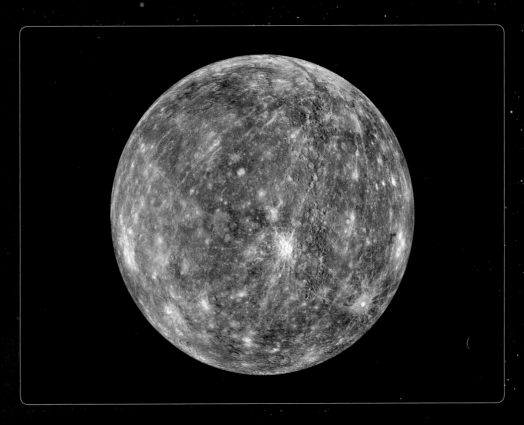

This photo of Mercury, taken in 2008 by Messenger, uses false color to highlight the many features of the planet's rocky surface.

UNPROTECTED

CHAPTER 5

Our Earth is surrounded by a protective blanket of gases called the **atmosphere**. Mercury formed in the same way and at the same time as Earth, but Mercury has no atmosphere.

A planet's atmosphere is held in place by its gravity. The planet's gravitational force stops the gases from floating off into space. Little Mercury's low gravity made it difficult for the planet to hold on to an atmosphere in the way that Earth has done.

Another factor in retaining an atmosphere is a planet's surface temperature. The hotter atmospheric gases become, the faster the gas **molecules** whiz around. Fast-moving gas molecules are even harder for a planet's gravity to hold in place!

Mercury's surface is extremely hot, so this combination of heat and low gravitational force meant that, unlike Earth, Mercury quickly lost most of its atmosphere.

*Mercury's surface is marked with many craters. Its thin atmosphere cannot protect it from **asteroid** impacts.*

MERCURY'S ORBIT AND ROTATION

CHAPTER 6

Earth orbits the Sun in a year, or once every 365 days. As it orbits, it also rotates on its **axis** once every 24 hours. We call this time period a day. Like Earth, Mercury also has years and days.

To orbit the Sun once, Earth must make a journey of nearly 560 million miles (900 million km). Because Mercury is much closer to the Sun, its journey is much shorter at 226 million miles (364 million km). Mercury is also a fast-moving planet. It travels through space at about 106,000 miles per hour (170,500 km/h), faster than Earth's speed of 67,000 miles per hour (108,000 km/h). This all adds up to Mercury making one orbit of the Sun every 88 days. So a year on Mercury is just 88 Earth days long.

Mercury, however, rotates on its own axis much slower than Earth. It takes Mercury nearly 59

Earth days to make just one rotation. So a day on Mercury lasts 59 days.

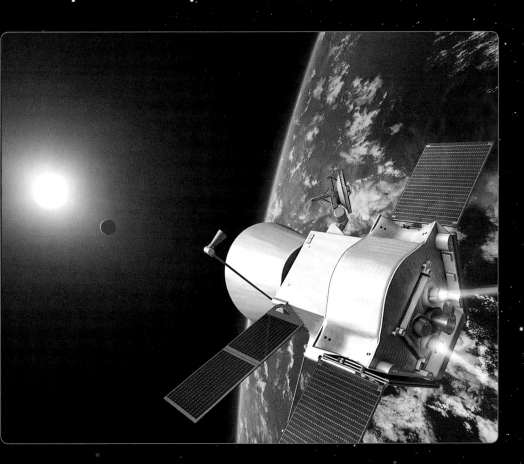

This illustration shows the European Space Agency's BepiColombo spacecraft on the way to Mercury. The small planet can be seen closely orbiting the Sun.

THE FIRST SIGHTINGS

CHAPTER 7

Because Mercury can be seen in the sky with the naked eye, people have known about it for thousands of years.

From Earth, Mercury is visible just after sunset or just before sunrise. The ancient Greeks actually believed it was two different stars. They named the evening star Hermes, the Greek name for the god the Romans called Mercury. They named the morning star Apollo after the Greek god of music, healing, and the Sun. It wasn't until around 350 BC that ancient Greek **astronomers** realized Mercury was a single planet and not two stars.

In 1631, French astronomer Pierre Gassendi used a telescope to watch Mercury pass in front of the Sun. He was the first person to witness the transit of a planet across the Sun.

For centuries, astronomers watched Mercury from Earth through telescopes. Then, in 1973, a spacecraft blasted off from Earth that would bring the world incredible close-up images of the closest planet to the Sun.

Mercury can be seen from Earth with the naked eye. In this photo, it is the second bright dot from the top. The brighest object is Venus.

MARINER 10

CHAPTER 8

On November 3, 1973, NASA's *Mariner 10* spacecraft blasted off from Cape Canaveral Air Force Station in Florida. The mission of the robotic spacecraft was to discover information about Venus and Mercury.

On February 5, 1974, *Mariner 10* flew past Venus, sending data and over 4,000 photos back to Earth. *Mariner 10* then used Venus's gravity to adjust its speed and **trajectory** so that it headed toward Mercury. It was the first spacecraft to use the gravity of one planet as a "slingshot" to assist its journey to another.

In March 1974, *Mariner 10* reached Mercury. The spacecraft made three flybys of the planet, taking photographs and collecting data. The photos it sent back to Earth showed a battered, rocky landscape not unlike the surface of the Moon.

On March 24, 1975, with its mission complete, *Mariner 10*'s contact with Earth was shut down.

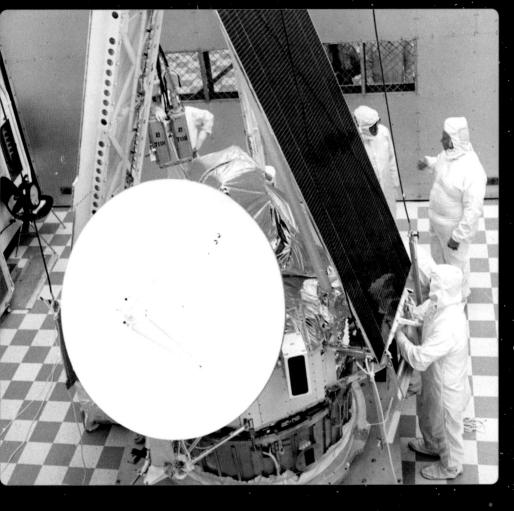

Mariner 10 *used **solar panels** to supply it with energy as it explored the planets of the inner solar system.*

FURTHER EXPLORATION

CHAPTER 9

Nearly 30 years after *Mariner 10* blasted off for Mercury, another spacecraft left Earth heading for the little planet.

On August 3, 2004, *Messenger* was launched from Cape Canaveral Air Force Station in Florida. *Messenger*'s mission was to orbit Mercury and find out more about the planet's core, surface, and **geologic history**. On board the spacecraft were many scientific instruments for collecting data. *Messenger* was also fitted with solar panels to capture sunlight and use it to power the spacecraft. Solar power could also be stored in an onboard battery.

Mercury's earlier visitor, *Mariner 10*, was designed to fly by the planet. *Messenger*, however, would be orbiting the planet and experiencing the intense heat of the Sun for a long period of time. In order to enable the spacecraft to operate in the extreme temperatures close to Mercury, *Messenger* was fitted with a protective sunshade.

Both powered by and protected from the Sun, *Messenger* left Earth's atmosphere ready to continue the work begun by *Mariner 10* three decades before.

Messenger celebrated its 10-year anniversary in August 2014. In its decade of exploration, the spacecraft has traveled over 8 billion miles (12 billion km).

EXPLORING MERCURY'S LANDSCAPE

CHAPTER 10

Reaching Mercury and then entering into orbit around the planet required that *Messenger* make a long and complex journey.

As *Messenger* got closer to Mercury and its giant neighbor the Sun, the Sun's powerful gravity caused the spacecraft to accelerate faster and faster. *Messenger* had to slow down enough to match Mercury's speed and allow the planet's weak gravity to capture it and pull it into orbit. In order to achieve the right speed and trajectory, *Messenger* had to make two flybys of Venus and then three flybys of Mercury. This complicated journey took six and a half years, but finally, in March 2011, *Messenger* went into orbit around Mercury.

Mariner 10 had captured images of about 45 percent of the planet's surface. One of *Messenger's* goals was to send back imagery of places not seen before. Now, thanks to *Messenger*, we've been able to see incredible images of huge cliffs, craters, and vast, deep impact basins caused by objects from space crashing into the planet.

This is Mariner 10's *first photo of Mercury, taken in 1974.*

A CRATERED SURFACE

CHAPTER 11

Almost since it formed about 4.6 billion years ago, Mercury has been bombarded by asteroids, **meteoroids**, and **comets**.

It's the same for all the planets in the solar system. They all regularly collide with both small and massive chunks of space debris. Mercury, however, has no protective atmosphere to shield it from these impacts. When small objects such as meteoroids head for Earth, they burn up in our atmosphere or our atmosphere causes them to break into smaller, less damaging pieces. On Mercury, they hit the planet's surface intact and at full speed!

Billions of years of impacts have left Mercury's surface covered with small craters, large craters, and truly vast craters, known as impact basins.

Mercury is home to one of the solar system's largest impact basins, the Caloris Basin. This huge feature on the planet's surface was formed early in Mercury's life, when it was hit by a giant asteroid.

This photo mosaic was taken by Mariner 10 and shows the cratered surface of Mercury.

FINDING ICE

CHAPTER 12

One of *Messenger*'s most amazing discoveries was the presence of ice on Mercury.

When scientists on Earth bounced radio waves off Mercury, they saw unexpectedly bright reflections from some places on the planet's surface. They thought these bright areas could be a particularly reflective type of rock. Another theory, however, was that the bright areas were ice.

In 2011, instruments on board *Messenger* confirmed that these bright areas are indeed pure frozen water. In fact, there could be up to one trillion tons (907 billion mt) of ice on the planet.

It seems unbelievable that ice could exist in one of the hottest places in the solar system. However, at the bottom of deep craters at

Mercury's north and south poles, there are dark, extremely cold places that are never touched by the Sun's light and heat.

No one knows for sure how the ice came to be on Mercury. One theory is that it could have come from comets, which are mostly made of ice, that collided with the planet.

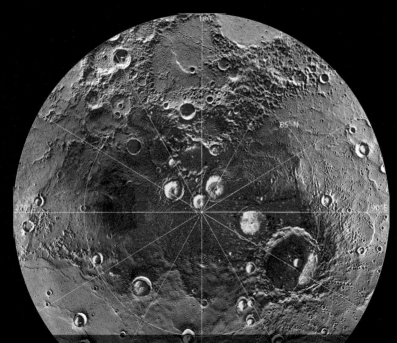

This photo shows Mercury's north pole. Red was added to show the shadowed craters of the planet where ice can exist.

WHAT WILL HAPPEN TO MERCURY?

CHAPTER 13

Mercury will not be around forever. In about five billion years, little Mercury's life will likely come to an end!

Stars like our Sun may burn for billions of years. Eventually, however, their supply of fuel burns out. As the Sun's supply of hydrogen fuel runs out, the star will swell in size to become what is known as a red giant. As the Sun swells, its already vast diameter will actually increase by up to 250 times. As it swells, the Sun will swallow up Mercury, bringing its time in space to a fiery end. Mercury's nearest neighbors, Venus and Earth, will also be engulfed by the dying Sun.

After about a billion years, the Sun will begin to expel, or blow off, its outer layers. These layers of gas and dust will form a nebula. Finally, the remains of the Sun's core will collapse, leaving just a small, dense star called a white dwarf. Then, all the chemical ingredients that were once the Sun, Mercury, and its planetary neighbors will be floating in a giant cloud ready to become part of a new star or planet.

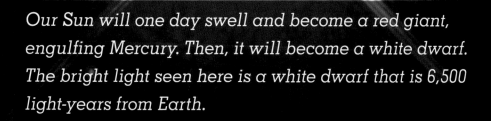

Our Sun will one day swell and become a red giant, engulfing Mercury. Then, it will become a white dwarf. The bright light seen here is a white dwarf that is 6,500 light-years from Earth.

29

GLOSSARY

asteroid: A small, rocky, planet-like body in space that circles the Sun.

astronomer: A person who studies stars, planets, and other heavenly bodies.

atmosphere: The gases that surround a planet.

axis: An imaginary line through the center of an object, around which the object rotates.

comet: A body in space made up of dust, gas, and ice that orbits the Sun. It sometimes develops a bright, long tail.

dwarf planet: A large body in space that orbits the Sun, but isn't large enough to be called a planet.

geologic history: The history of a planet as recorded in its rocks.

gravity: The attraction of the mass of a body in space for other bodies nearby.

mass: The amount of matter in something.

meteoroid: A piece of rocky or metal-like matter traveling through space.

molecule: A very small piece of matter.

molten: Turned to liquid by heat.

nebula: A huge cloud of dust and gas found between stars.

orbit: To travel in a circle or oval path around something.

planet: A large body in space that has its own motion around the Sun or another star.

solar panel: A panel of cells that change energy from the Sun into electricity.

solar system: The Sun and the space bodies that move around it, including the planets and their moons.

trajectory: The curved path along which something moves through the air or space.

FOR MORE INFORMATION

BOOKS

Aguilar, David A. *13 Planets: The Latest View of the Solar System.* Washington, D.C.: National Geographic, 2011.

Sparrow, Giles. *Destination Mercury.* New York, NY: PowerKids, 2010.

Squire, Ann O. *Planet Mercury.* New York, NY: Children's Press, 2014.

WEBSITES

Due to the changing nature of Internet links, PowerKids Press has developed an online list of websites related to the subject of this book. This site is updated regularly. Please use this link to access the list: www.powerkidslinks.com/soss/merc

INDEX